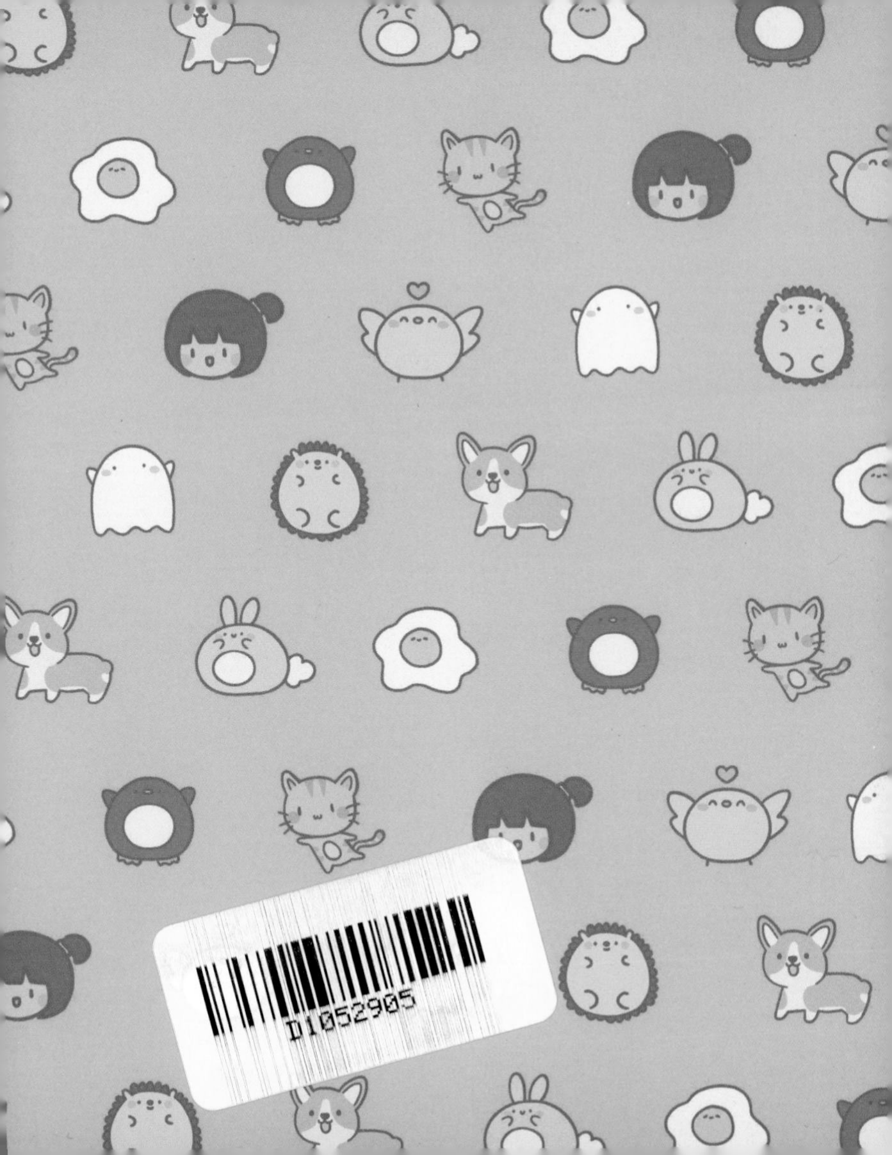

# Loading
# Penguin Hugs

hug sent! ♥

# Loading Penguin Hugs

## heartwarming comics from chibird

Jacqueline Chen

Andrews McMeel
PUBLISHING®

# ghost hug!

## you can't feel it, but it's there!

# reasons to get out of bed

the sun is
shining for you

pet
pet

there are puppies
to pet

ice cream
flavors to try

new books
to read

and a lot of steps
forward to take

# YES, you can do it!

# NO, it won't be easy, but it'll be worth it!

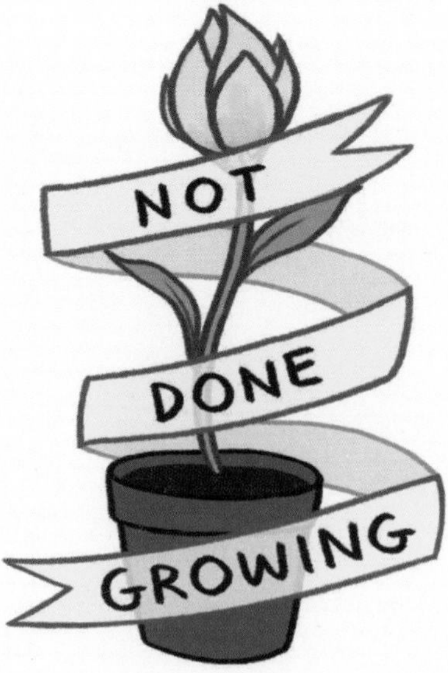
NOT
DONE
GROWING

I should be
more active.

I should eat
healthier.

I should be more
thick skinned.

I should realize this
all takes time,

and I'll get there
step-by-step.

will he do it?

life is tough.

but so are you!

you are SMARTER than you think.
you are STRONGER than you think.

you are capable of so much
MORE than you think.

this little hedgehog thinks
you're doing a good job.

she wants you to keep it up!

today I will not insult myself.

no, it's a good one!

when something sad happens,
it's hard to bounce back immediately.

take some time to be sad.

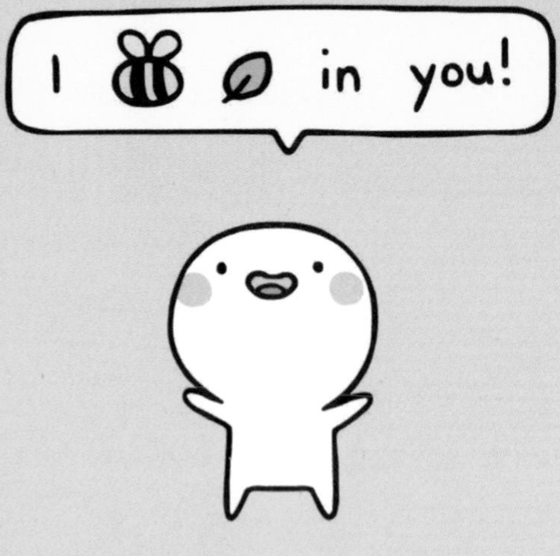
I in you!

instead of focusing on the negative,

try to remember all the things
you're grateful for instead.

# positive puppers

🦴

it's tough, but you're
doing amazing!!!

keep up all the
good work, friend!

you're not alone!
I'm here for you!

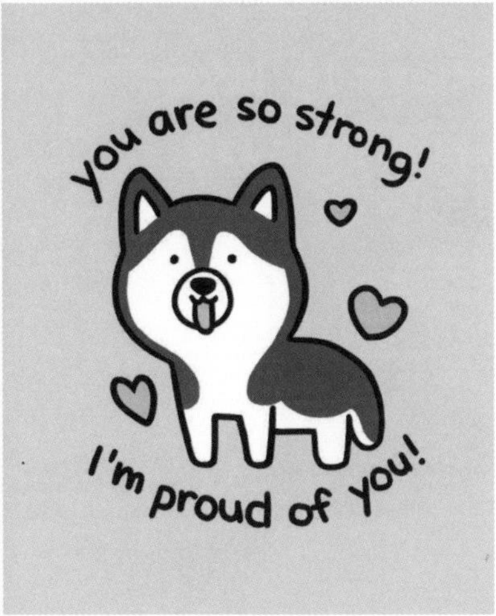
you are so strong!
I'm proud of you!

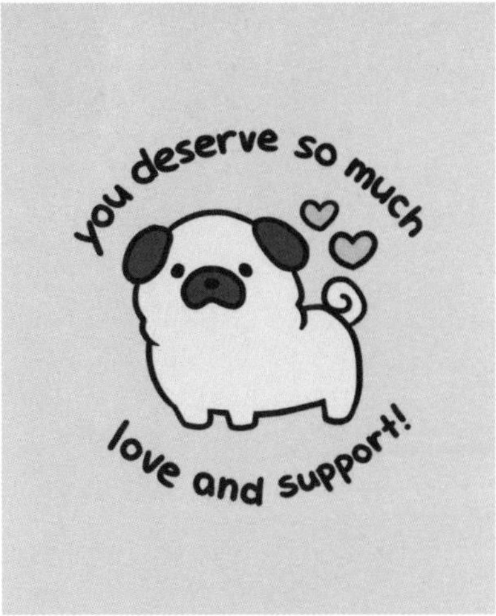
you deserve so much
love and support!

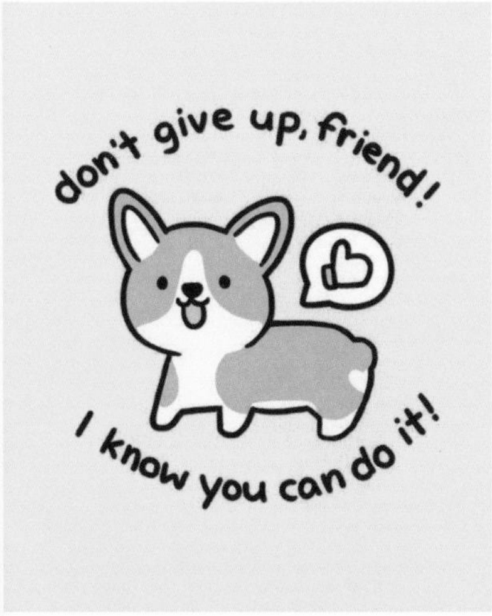
don't give up, friend!
I know you can do it!

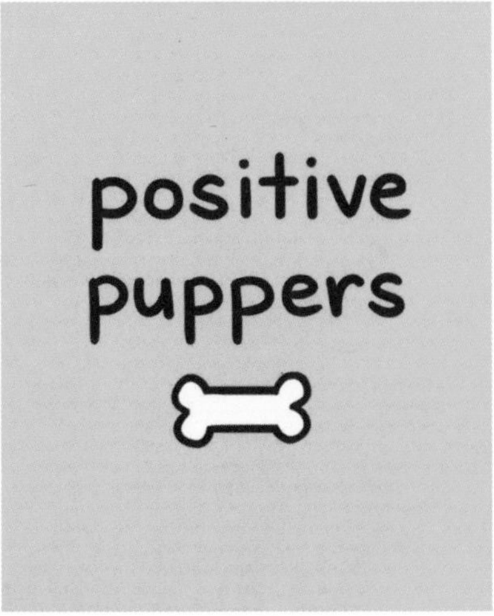
positive
puppers

oh, a text! I'll answer it later today when I'm not so busy.

A FEW DAYS LATER...

# things we all need more of

warm hugs

good sleep

adventures

interesting
conversations

laughter

happy dances

bad things <u>will</u> happen.

be someone who reacts positively
and makes the most out of it.

mosaic →

I hope you figure things out.

I hope you find wonderful people
to surround yourself with.

I hope you feel happy and loved.

you deserve all those things.

today I will be stronger.
today I will be kinder.
today I will grow.

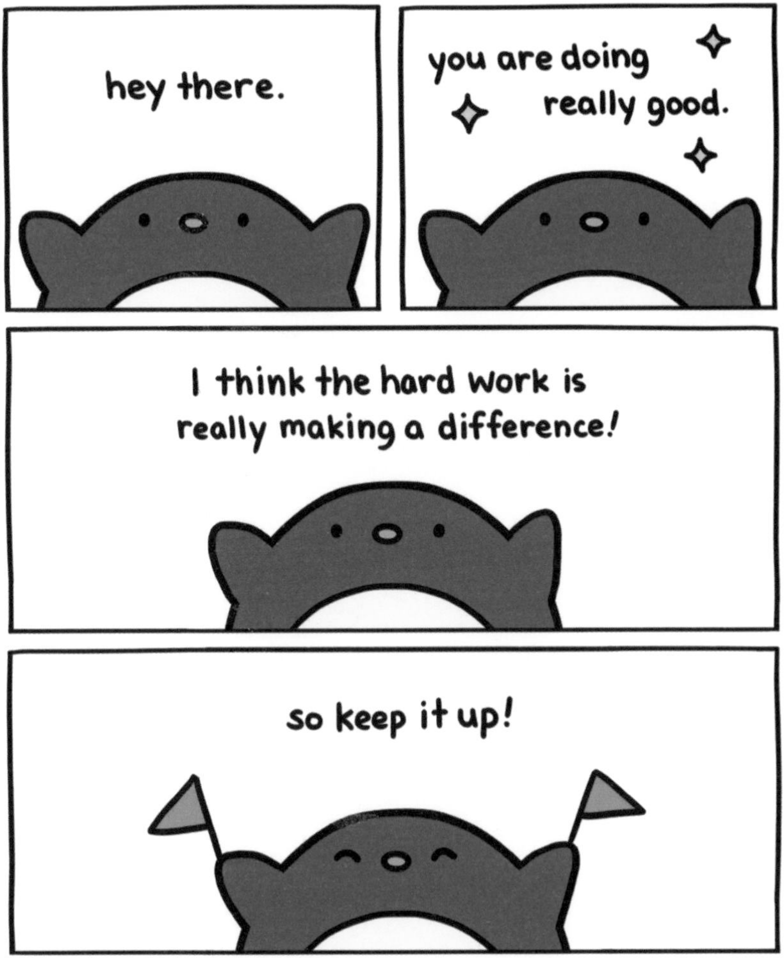
hey there.
you are doing really good.
I think the hard work is really making a difference!
so keep it up!

# different ways to be kind to yourself

compliment yourself

make yourself
tea/coffee

reach out when
you need help

let yourself be sad
if you need to be

treat yourself every so often

guess what?

you're a cutie-pie!

# stop comparing yourself to others.

"prettier" "smarter"
"funnier" "kinder"

awesome

also
awesome

maybe I <u>am</u> a lazy bum. but at least
I've accepted it and moved on.

a lot of people only get support <u>after</u> they accomplish something awesome.

I'm here to support you before that. go you!!!

# old me

I'm trash.

# new me

I'm AWESOME trash.

not everyone's path takes
the same amount of time.

it's ok if you progress slower!
everyone's journey is different.

don't forget about your past
accomplishments!

they were amazing back then,
and they're still amazing now!

have an egg-cellent day!

I hope it's eggs-tra good!

I will believe in you

even when you have trouble
believing in yourself.

I know you are tired and sad

don't worry, little one

with a little time and love,
things will get better

you are so brave for making it this far.
keep fighting, adventurer!

you can be happy.
don't give up on
yourself like that.
I see a lot of happiness
in your future. please
keep fighting for it.
you CAN do it.

positive bunny

whenever you are struggling,
remember the times you have
succeeded and survived, and know
that you can make it through.

positive bunny

you are not a failure.
you are still growing.
don't feel bad about that.

positive bunny

you are enough.

and that's all you need to be.

# if life had power-ups

negativity shield   confidence boost   double focus

motivation boost   stress shield   energy boost

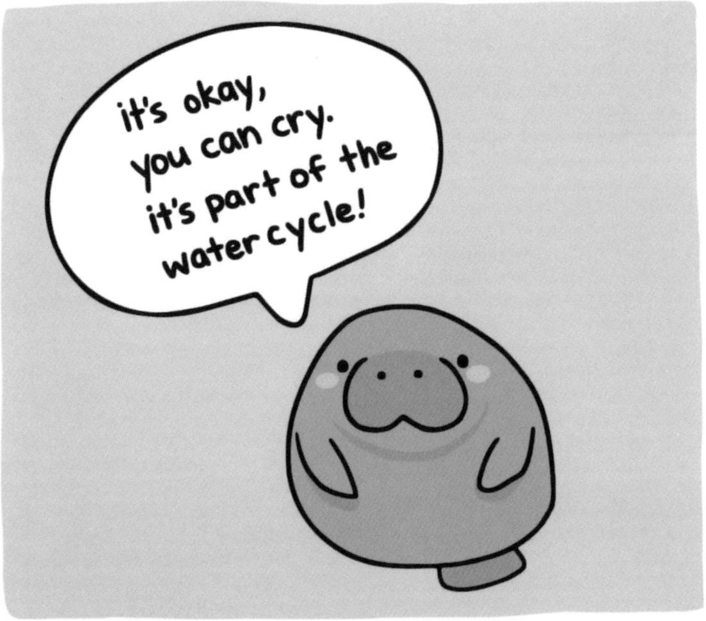
it's okay, you can cry. it's part of the water cycle!

# your definition of a good day will look different from other people's

slept 6+ hours
cleaned room
took a walk

finished 2 tasks in the morning
scheduled next week
high productivity

hung out with friends
laughed a lot
full of food

read a book
learned a cool fact
didn't worry too much

I have no idea what I'm doing,

but I'm gonna figure it out!

# thankful for best friends who

get all your
inside jokes

don't need explanation
because they already know

don't believe in
"too much information"

are still best friends
despite long distance

look out!!!

there's a really cute person!
(it's you!)

# RULE 1 : BE NICE TO OTHERS

# RULE 2: BE NICE TO YOURSELF

YOU ARE NOT UGLY.
YOU ARE NOT STUPID.
YOU ARE DOING GREAT!

don't get discouraged!
things take a while to change.

keep at it – I know they'll
change for the better for you!

thank you to all my emotions,
not just the positive ones.

the negative ones tell you when
something's wrong and needs to
change, and that's really important.

it may look like I'm doing well and
have my life together.
I just want you to know...

that is a straight-up lie.

it's going to be okay.

you're going to be okay.

# good reasons to be positive

it makes others
around you happy

more intrinsic
motivation

less stress
and worry

you notice
more good things

today was not great...

but tomorrow might be!

even if you only find a little bit
of happiness each day,

those happinesses add up!

I am so strong and don't need anyone's help!

(but I can still get help sometimes.)

ramen can be instant.
successes usually aren't.

don't be upset if it's slow.
your hard work and dedication <u>matter.</u>

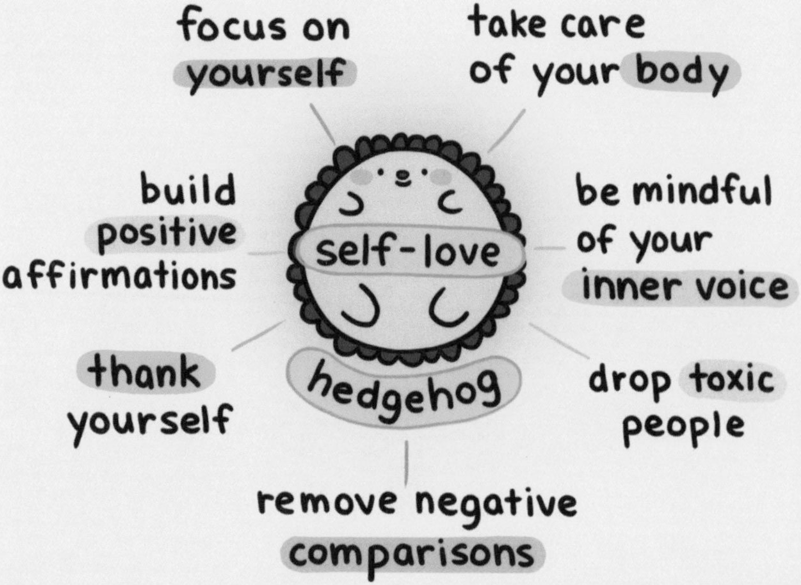
focus on yourself
take care of your body
build positive affirmations
self-love
be mindful of your inner voice
thank yourself
hedgehog
drop toxic people
remove negative comparisons

friend: hey wanna
go out tonight?

20%

current
energy

40%

energy required
to go out and
have a good time

nah I'm good,
but thanks!

# penguin of determination

I'm going to be ok.

I'll work it out.

I'll keep moving forward.

I'll never give up.

hi, we're
your flaws. and we're
your strengths!

together,
we balance —

I'M THE WORST
PERSON EVER.

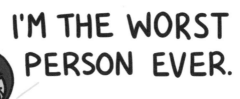

## FRIENDLY REMINDER:

You are **not weak** for asking for help.

You are **not dumb** for not knowing things.

You are **not selfish** for wanting better than what you have now.

when you're done for the day
and can finally relax.

ahh.

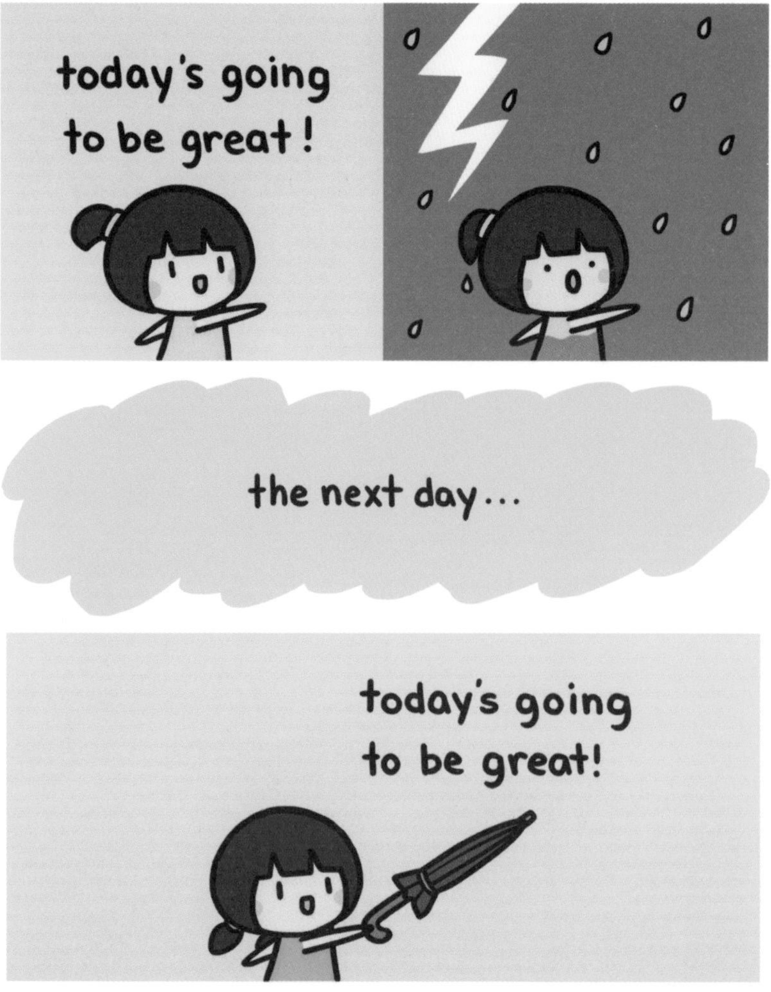
today's going to be great!
the next day...
today's going to be great!

even when you've lost all hope,

please don't give up.

be someone your future self would be proud of.

never stop fighting.
your storm could be over soon.

we often assume we have to
do it all alone.

but that's not true! people care
about you and want you to succeed.

you just have to find them
and keep them close.

no one said you can't
be cute AND powerful.

never give up on your dreams!

you'll find a way to make it happen.

things are going to
work out for you.

maybe differently than you
expected, but that's okay.

## YOU JUST GOT:

1 order of happiness with a side
of smiles and extra sunshine!

thank you! please come again!

# BEST feelings

when someone remembers
a small detail about you

naturally waking
up refreshed

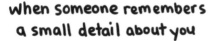

taking the first bite
when you're really hungry

perfect high fives

sometimes you get dealt bad cards.

it's all about how you use them.

it's okay to be tired.
don't feel guilty about it!

you're not expected to have
infinite energy.

don't be disappointed by a slow recovery. all good things take time.

you're a lot tougher than you were
a few years ago. every challenge
makes you stronger.

old
challenges →

new
challenges
↓

will tea fix all my problems?

no, but it certainly makes
me feel better.

Why are you so happy today?

I made brief contact
with a dog!

turn your dreams
into <u>plans</u>.

# reasons NOT to be lazy today

you'll feel good
about yourself

the rest will be
easier after starting

if not today,
then when?

one step closer
to your goals

there is never a better time
to grow than now.

you are loved.

today, tomorrow, and forever.

your story isn't finished yet.

write your own ending.

# Index

# Acknowledgments

Thank you to my family, Ying Wang, Gary Chen, and Katherine Chen, for the love that made me who I am today.

A special thank you to Peter Koutras, who never stopped supporting me. I am eternally grateful for all the times you made me dinner so I had more time to draw, gave me motivation when I thought I had run out, and did everything apart from drawing the actual comics themselves. You deserve so many wafers!

Many thanks to my friends, especially Julia and Ge, for the encouragement through tough times and the answers to my constant indecisiveness. I don't know how many times you all have helped me through my "I don't know" moments.

Thank you to Kathleen Ortiz, my wonderful agent who helped bring this book to life.

And as always, thank you to all my followers who have supported my art and cheered me on for years. You all believed in me so much that I started believing in myself too.

# About the Author

**Jacqueline Chen** has been drawing motivational comics and animations since high school, cheering up millions of people along the way. When she's not making art, she's coding, designing, and playing video games. She loves ice cream and bubble tea a little too much.

Find more cheerful drawings from the world of Chibird on chibird.com and @chibirdart on Instagram or Facebook.

Andrews McMeel Publishing
a division of Andrews McMeel Universal
1130 Walnut Street, Kansas City, Missouri 64106

www.andrewsmcmeel.com

18 19 20 21 22 RLP 10 9 8 7 6 5 4 3 2 1

ISBN: 978-1-4494-9458-2

Library of Congress Control Number: 2018938764

Editor: Patty Rice
Designer, Art Director: Julie Barnes
Production Editor: Elizabeth A. Garcia
Production Manager: Tamara Haus

ATTENTION: SCHOOLS AND BUSINESSES
Andrews McMeel books are available at quantity discounts with
bulk purchase for educational, business, or sales promotional use.
For information, please e-mail the Andrews McMeel Publishing
Special Sales Department: specialsales@amuniversal.com.